SEX LIVES OF OUR PARENTS

Michael Mitnick

BROADWAY PLAY PUBLISHING INC
224 E 62nd St, NY, NY 10065
www.broadwayplaypub.com
info@broadwayplaypub.com

SEX LIVES OF OUR PARENTS
© Copyright 2014 by Michael Mitnick

First printing: February 2014
I S B N: 978-0-88145-575-5

Book design: Marie Donovan
Page make-up: Adobe Indesign
Typeface: Palatino
Printed and bound in the U S A

SEX LIVES OF OUR PARENTS was first produced by Second Stage Theatre (Casey Reitz, Executive Director; Carole Rothman, Artistic Director; Christopher Burney, Associate Artistic Director and 2ST Uptown Curator), opening on 22 June 2011. The cast and creative contributor were:

ELLIOT.. Teddy Bergman
CHARLOTTE ....Lisa Emery
CHRISTOPHER... Daniel Jenkins
VIRGINIA..Virginia Kull
JEFF.. Ben Rappaport
LUCAS .... Mark Zeisler

Director..Davis McCallum
Assistant director..............................Zach Chotzen-Freund
Set designer...................................... Andromache Chalfant
Costume designer..Jessica Ford
Lighting designer .... Tyler Micoleau
Sound designer..Jill BC Du Boff
Assistant costume designer ....Kim Newton
Assistant lighting designer...............................Marika Kent
Assistant sound designer..................................Janie Bullard
General manager..................................... Dean A Carpenter
Press representative .... The Hartman Group
Production stage manager .... Winnie Y Lok
Stage manager.. McKenzie Murphy
Production manager ....Jeff Wild
Technical director............................... Robert G Mahon III
Prop master..Susan Barras
Wardrobe.. Cornelia Wall
Casting... MelCap Casting

The play was later developed by Washington Ensemble Theatre and ACT Seattle, in April of 2013, directed by Ali el-Gasseir.

CHARACTERS & SETTING

Jeff
Virginia
Elliot
Charlotte
Christopher
Lucas
Nurse

Doubling: Elliot / Nurse

Time & Place:
The Second Half of the Twentieth Century
Locations in the Northeast

Prologue:
Ballet

(Cue the orchestra!)

(If I Had You, sung by Frank Sinatra plays.)

(A library)

(Lights up on JEFF, *reading He turns pages, bored.)*

(Enter VIRGINIA, *wearing a bookbag and an S L R camera to her side. She carries an armload of library books. She holds a scrap of paper, passing before us, squinting at the spines on an unseen bookshelf.)*

*(*JEFF *looks up as she passes. He follows her with his eyes.)*

(She exits.)

(After a moment, JEFF *returns to his book.)*

*****

(The campus quad)

*(*VIRGINIA *enters, wearing a large pair of headphones. She carries her bookbag, which is half unzipped as well as her camera. An orange sweatshirt is sticking out of the bag's opening.)*

(JEFF *enters from the opposite side, walking with* ELLIOT. *As* JEFF *notices* VIRGINIA, JEFF *stops walking.* ELLIOT *continues. After a few steps,* ELLIOT *turns back to* JEFF *and shrugs, as if to say, "Hey, why'd you stop, Jeff?".)*

(JEFF *motions— "Keep going—I'll meet up with you later, Elliot.")*

(VIRGINIA *kneels down to take a photo, placing her bookbag beside her.* JEFF *sneaks up, unseen, and steals the sweatshirt from her bookbag. She finishes tying her shoe, picks up her bookbag, and stands. She starts to exit when he runs up to her, tapping her on the shoulder. She jumps, surprised.)*

(JEFF *holds out her sweatshirt, mouthing, "You dropped this."* VIRGINIA *smiles. He points to himself and says, "I'm Jeff". He shakes her hand.)*

VIRGINIA: *(Mouthed shouting, unaware of the "level" of her voice)* I'm Virginia!

(JEFF *laughs as* VIRGINIA *pulls off her headphones, embarrassed. He puts the headphones back on her head. He pantomimes— "Want to get a drink with me?"* VIRGINIA *smiles and points to her watch. Then the sun. It's early.* JEFF *waves away that notion, reiterating, "Want to get a drink with me?")*

(VIRGINIA *hesitates, then relents.)*

(VIRGINIA *and* JEFF *exit back in the direction from which she had entered.)*

*****

(A movie theater.)

(JEFF *and* VIRGINIA *watch a movie. They share a bucket of popcorn.)*

*****

(JEFF *poses for a photo. He sucks on his finger.* VIRGINIA *lowers the camera, mock-disgusted. He gives a cheesy smile. She snaps.*)

******

(An important meeting.)

(VIRGINIA *introduces* JEFF *to her parents,* CHARLOTTE *and* CHRISTOPHER. JEFF *wears a tie.*)

(Introductions are made. CHARLOTTE *laughs, patting* JEFF'*s tie. He shrugs.)*

(CHARLOTTE *shows off her new skirt. She spins, and it billows.*)

(JEFF *stares, mesmerized by her legs.*)

(CHRISTOPHER *watches* JEFF'*s ogling. He snaps his fingers in front of* JEFF'*s eyes.* JEFF *looks up.* CHARLOTTE *playfully pushes* CHRISTOPHER.)

*****

(A dance)

(VIRGINIA *and* JEFF *slow dance. They rest their foreheads against each other.*)

(The seasons change.)

(Fall)

(Winter)

(Spring)

(Graduation— They toss mortarboards!)

*(*JEFF *kneels to tie his shoelace.* VIRGINIA *turns away a moment, to prepare her camera for a photo. When she turns back,* JEFF *is holding out an open ring box.)*

(Their eyes meet.)

*(*VIRGINIA *smiles and mouths "sure".)*

*(*JEFF *picks her up and spins her around.)*

(They kiss as the song concludes.)

(On the final brass "bump", the lights go out.)

1

(Lights up on JEFF *and* VIRGINIA, *sleeping in her childhood bed.* VIRGINIA *bolts upright.)*

*(*VIRGINIA *rubs her sweat-covered face. She gets out of bed and exits off. After a few more moments, we hear a toilet flush. And the sound of a faucet running. She reenters, carrying a wet washcloth which she pats on her forehead. She walks over to a floor fan and turns it on full blast. She lifts her long T-Shirt, flashing the fan.)*

VIRGINIA: Ohhhh.
(Turning to him)
Jeff?
Jeff?

JEFF: Mmmm.

*(*VIRGINIA *walks over the bed and pushes* JEFF's *shoulder.)*

JEFF: Mmmm.

*(*VIRGINIA *hits* JEFF's *back, hard.)*

JEFF: Owww!
Did you just hit me?

VIRGINIA: You're awake too?

JEFF: What's wrong?

VIRGINIA: I had a nightmare.

(JEFF sits up and rubs his eyes.)

JEFF: Well I was having a great dream. I dreamt I won the Winter Olympics. The whole thing.

(JEFF sees that VIRGINIA is genuinely upset.)

JEFF: What's wrong?

VIRGINIA: It's stupid.

(A moment)

JEFF: So…should I just go back to bed or—

VIRGINIA: I'm sorry I woke you up.

JEFF: It's fine.
(He leans back down.)

VIRGINIA: So, I was dreaming—

JEFF: And she's talking.
(Sitting back up)

VIRGINIA: I dreamt that I could see my mom.

(On a nearby bench, CHARLOTTE appears. She sits backwards. We don't see her face.)

VIRGINIA: And, she was sitting on a bench.

JEFF: That's a fucked up dream.

(VIRGINIA laughs and hits JEFF.)

VIRGINIA: She was sitting next to a man.

(A man sits down on the bench. We don't see his face.)

VIRGINIA: I couldn't see their faces.
But I could see that my Mom was, like, leaning over and…kissing this man's neck.

(On the bench, CHARLOTTE kisses the man.)

VIRGINIA: And the man wasn't my Dad.
Annnnnd…that was it.

(Suddenly, the bench and the people vanish.)

JEFF: Well. That. Is. Troubling. To you.

VIRGINIA: Yeah.

JEFF: So your Mom was having an affair or—

VIRGINIA: No, it was a long time ago. I knew that much.
It was a long time ago.
But the whole thing felt so much more real than a
dream. I've never…

(Silence)

JEFF: It's probably just because you're sleeping in your
childhood bedroom and your folks are down the hall.

VIRGINIA: Maybe.

JEFF: Cool.

VIRGINIA: What's cool about it?

JEFF: Nothing. It was automatic. I'm not really firing on
all cylinders.

VIRGINIA: I don't know why I'm so upset. I hate when
people talk about dreams.

JEFF: Me too.
(Silence)
Since we're both up…you wanna do it?

VIRGINIA: Do what?

JEFF: Like, in the bed where you grew up.

VIRGINIA: Ew, Jeff.

JEFF: What? I just think it would be funny.

VIRGINIA: I need to take a shower. I'm covered in sweat. Sorry I woke you up.
(She exits to the bathroom.)

JEFF: Are your grandparents coming to the wedding?

VIRGINIA: *(Off)* They're dead, Jeff.

JEFF: *(To himself)* Oh yeah.

(Sound of the shower starting)

JEFF: So I guess not.

(Blackout)

2

(The home of CHARLOTTE *and* CHRISTOPHER*)*

*(*CHARLOTTE, CHRISTOPHER, VIRGINIA, *and* JEFF *are sampling potential desserts intended for the wedding dinner.)*

*(*CHRISTOPHER's *pants are unbuckled.)*

(He sits back with his hands folded on this stomach.)

*(*VIRGINIA *pours herself a glass of wine.)*

*(*JEFF *is finishing* VIRGINIA's *dessert.)*

CHRISTOPHER: Oh I love this. It's so smooth. Like shaving cream.

VIRGINIA: *(To* JEFF*)* You're getting it on your pants.

JEFF: Mmmmm.

CHARLOTTE: Slow down there, Jeff, or you'll find yourself looking like him.
(She points to CHRISTOPHER.)*

CHRISTOPHER: *(Patting his round stomach)* What's wrong with this??

CHARLOTTE: Oh nothing.
It just looks like you'll be   CHRISTOPHER:
giving me grandchildren   Charlotte...
before Virginia.

VIRGINIA: Mom...

JEFF: *(With mouth full)*
Grandchildren? He'd be giving you a regular child if
he's your husband.

CHARLOTTE: Well, all my children are grand. Especially
that one right there.

CHRISTOPHER: Virginia's her favorite.

VIRGINIA: Shhhh you!

CHRISTOPHER: She *is*.

VIRGINIA: Everyone's favorite is Lucas.

JEFF:
Luke is my favorite.   CHRISTOPHER:
                               Which one is Luke again?

CHARLOTTE:
Looks like your favorite is   CHRISTOPHER:
the peach cobbler.   Would you stop calling
                               me fat?

CHARLOTTE: I'm not calling   CHRISTOPHER: Oh-ho. Yes
you fat. I'm *saying* you wish you are. You think I'm a
you had married a pastry   big fatty. Jeff—I still
chef instead of a—   weigh—I do wish I
                               married a pastry chef. I
                               wish you were a pastry
                               chef.

JEFF: It's incredible. At least half butter.

VIRGINIA: We need a non-dairy option.

CHARLOTTE: We also need a non-gluten option.

JEFF: What's gluten?

CHRISTOPHER: *(To* JEFF*)* Oh all these trends. No dairy. No gluten. No Only eggs. Only No…pimentos. Only organic, humanely slaughtered *pimentos.* Cage free pimentos…

CHARLOTTE: Pimentos? What is he— Christopher, what are you talking about?

VIRGINIA: He's talking about pimentos again.

JEFF: What about the chocolate almond torte?

(VIRGINIA *pours herself another glass of wine.)*

CHARLOTTE: *(Checking a little notecard)* Also dairy.

CHRISTOPHER: I like the cheesecake.

VIRGINIA: You like them all.

CHRISTOPHER: Is the cheesecake dairy?

(The women glare at CHRISTOPHER.*)*

CHRISTOPHER: Watch out, Jeff, these women stop laughing the moment they know they got you.

CHARLOTTE & VIRGINIA: Not true!

CHRISTOPHER: See my wife's plate? She always leaves one bite of every dessert, like an offering to the Gods. Like that one bite will make up for the fact that she just ate twelve thousand calories.

(He stands and starts to exit. His pants fall down.)

VIRGINIA: *(Covering her eyes)* Daddy!

CHRISTOPHER: What? I undid the uh-whatsit

CHARLOTTE: Buckle!	VIRGINIA: *(Eyes closed)*
JEFF: No. They're not—	Are they up yet? Daddy, would please this is so
CHRISTOPHER: Child services? You're an old maid now. Out toooooo pasture.	inappropriate. I should call child services.

CHARLOTTE: *(Sternly)* Christopher! Pull. Up. Your. Pants!

(CHRISTOPHER *pulls up his pants and exits.*)

CHARLOTTE: That's how you have to talk to children.

VIRGINIA: Ohhhh enough with the talk of children.

CHARLOTTE: What?

VIRGINIA: You think you're so subtle. *(Mocking)* "I don't know what you're talking about…"	CHARLOTTE: I don't know what you're talking about. Sheez. Louise.

(CHRISTOPHER *returns holding a fancy bottle of Champagne.*)

JEFF: I'm sterile anyway.

(An awkward pause)

VIRGINIA: He's joking.

CHRISTOPHER: *(Stonefaced)* How would you know?

(VIRGINIA sighs and pours herself a third glass.)

CHARLOTTE: Easy, honey. Dad bought nice champagne.

(CHRISTOPHER opens the bottle of champagne.)

VIRGINIA: I don't want it.

CHRISTOPHER: Then you can just toast with it.
Here we go— Bombs away!

(The champagne pops.)

(VIRGINIA yelps.)

(They all look at her.)

CHRISTOPHER: *(Pouring glasses and distributing one-by-one)*
For Mama Bear.
And Papa Bear.
For Baby Bear.
And for…

JEFF: Jeff.

CHRISTOPHER: *(Raising his glass)* To true love.

CHARLOTTE: Here, here.

JEFF: *(To VIRGINIA, hushed)* Raise your glass.

(They clink glasses and sip.)

(VIRGINIA is distracted.)

JEFF: You're both so kind to open your home to us.

VIRGINIA: It's my home. I lived here all my life.

CHARLOTTE: Well so did I. So there. We're the same.

JEFF: And you really don't have to wash the towels
after each shower—it's like a five star hotel around
here…

CHRISTOPHER: Hands off the chambermaid!

JEFF: Actually, I don't think I know how you guys met.

CHRISTOPHER: Virginia didn't tell you?

JEFF: No.

CHRISTOPHER: You didn't tell him the story?!
Virginia?

VIRGINIA: Hm?

CHARLOTTE: Oh it doesn't matter. Drop it…

CHRISTOPHER: I'm the true love of her life. She just
didn't know it. I had to ask her out fifteen times
before she said yes. In my day, that was called
"romantic courting". These days that's called "sexual
harassment".

CHARLOTTE: Believe me, I was this close to getting the
restraining order.

(The parents laugh.)

CHRISTOPHER: We met at Juilliard.

JEFF: You went to Juilliard too?

CHRISTOPHER: I played second kazoo.
No, I worked in the bookstore for beer money. I was at
City College.

(VIRGINIA pours yet another glass of wine.)

CHRISTOPHER: Her mother used to come in to buy sheet
music.

CHARLOTTE: French horn.

CHRISTOPHER: I saw this… The most beautiful girl I'd
ever seen in my entire life, thumbing through Haydn.
Mendelssohn. Schubert. Brahms.
I thought she was coming in just to see me.

CHARLOTTE: I was just coming in to buy sheet music.

CHRISTOPHER: It's a well-documented fact that pretty girls don't play French horns.
Honestly. You hear people say, "I looked at her and I *knew*."
Well I looked at her and I knew.
And so every time she came in, I'd say,

CHARLOTTE: "Lemme buy you dinner."

CHRISTOPHER: And she'd
say, "I have a boyfriend."   CHARLOTTE: Wouldn't
                                     leave me—

Oh I gave her discounts…
I gave her free reeds.

                                     French horns don't even
                                     need reeds.

I didn't know that…I didn't
know the first thing—

JEFF: She had a boyfriend! You had a boyfriend!

VIRGINIA: She didn't.

CHRISTOPHER: But she didn't! She just didn't want to go to dinner with me.

VIRGINIA: I can't imagine why…

CHRISTOPHER: It was such an elaborate lie, too. She named him…get this. Here's a name I never forgot: *Lucas Schroeder*. And he supposedly played the *piano*.

JEFF: Schroeder? Like the Charlie Brown—the Peanuts cartoon thing?

CHRISTOPHER: Lucas Schroeder. And she was madddddddly in love with him. Made up every last detail about him—this bookish, failed concert pianist. Cut the tendon in his pointer finger because some kid had hidden a razor blade between the keys of one of the practice pianos.

CHARLOTTE: Juilliard was a cutthroat place. *The point was* that Christopher...well, Christopher was a bit... overeager for my taste.

CHRISTOPHER: If you see something you want, you've got to grab it. Otherwise you spend a lifetime wishing you did.

JEFF: Do you still play the French horn?

CHARLOTTE: What's that?

> VIRGINIA: No. She doesn't.

CHARLOTTE: Yes I do!

VIRGINIA: You have it hanging over the fireplace like a piece of mass-produced folk art you got from The Pottery Barn.

CHRISTOPHER: Ginny, that's enough.

(Uncomfortable silence)

(An electronic beep)

JEFF: *FUCK!*
Oh shit. I mean. I'm sorry.
(He checks his BlackBerry.)

CHRISTOPHER: It's O K. Believe it or not, I've heard those words before.

VIRGINIA: What is it?

JEFF: *(To* VIRGINIA*)* Elliot's having his weekly meltdown. I've bumped it twice. I have to go.
(He stands up.)

CHARLOTTE:
Virginia's   VIRGINIA:

coworker friend?	Elliot was Jeff's roommate
No! No! He was your roommate? How didn't I know that? Why didn't I know that?	CHRISTOPHER: I knew that. I even remember that he's an alcoholic. And has a lisp! The lisping alcoholic!
No you didn't know that! He's making that up!	JEFF: Actually, Christopher's right.

JEFF: Sorry about…my language. That was. I'm trying really hard not to say anything wrong.

CHRISTOPHER: Maybe you should try to say something right.

VIRGINIA: You know, Mommy dearest, I don't think I've *EVER* heard you swear.
(*Silence*)
In twenty-two years, not one swear word.

JEFF: Um.

CHRISTOPHER: Coffee…table one please.

VIRGINIA: Say a swear word, Mom.

CHRISTOPHER: O K. Jeff, you're good to drive?

(*They all stand, except* VIRGINIA.)

JEFF: Yes, I only had two glasses. You don't like me much anyway, Chris. Who cares if I crash?

VIRGINIA: No. I want to hear Mom swear.
Say...*fuck.*
(Silence)
See—she won't do it!

CHARLOTTE:		
(Kissing his cheek) I'll tell Jesse that you loved the cobbler.	JEFF: *(To VIRGINIA)* Do you feel O K?	
		CHRISTOPHER:
	VIRGINIA: Everyone gets to make jokes except me.	Oh the cobbler was the best part.
Because I didn't		I love your cooking. Shush!

CHARLOTTE: Do you have the key to the house?

(JEFF pats his pocket.)

CHARLOTTE: The alarm is —

JEFF: 5, 2, 4 / 5, 2, 4.
(Picks up his bag.)

CHRISTOPHER: 5, 2, 4—May, 24th. The day after my birthday...

CHARLOTTE: ...Someone could look up his actual birthday. Using Internet.

CHRISTOPHER: Using *the* Internet.

CHARLOTTE: That's what I—

CHRISTOPHER: No. You said, "Using Internet". Like "Me Tarzan, You—"

CHARLOTTE: Oh shush...like you're so "with it"...

JEFF: I'm sorry about this.

(He kisses the top of VIRGINIA*'s head.)*

I'll be back before you know it.

*(*JEFF *exits. A door slams. A car door opens. Then slams. Car engine. Tires against gravel.)*

*(*VIRGINIA *sits, tracing the top of her wine glass with her fingertip.* CHARLOTTE *and* CHRISTOPHER *and stand a moment, silent, staring at their daughter.)*

CHRISTOPHER: …Well…I think I'll clear.

*(*CHRISTOPHER *gathers plates and exits.* CHARLOTTE *looks at the room.)*

CHARLOTTE: Do you think we should redo this room? It's the same wallpaper since when I was a little girl. I always wanted to change it but somehow I never did. Now this pattern is "in" again. What do you think?

VIRGINIA: I don't know. Maybe.

CHARLOTTE: Well, someday when this is your house you can design it any way you want.

VIRGINIA: Is this all life is?

(Long pause)

CHARLOTTE: Get some sleep.

*(*CHARLOTTE *clears more dishes, leaving* VIRGINIA*.)*

*(*VIRGINIA *takes a bite of the cobbler.)*

(Blackout)

3

(The same night.)

*(*ELLIOT *and* JEFF *sit in a bar.* ELLIOT *drinks seltzer,* JEFF*, a beer.* ELLIOT *has a little lisp.)*

JEFF: This morning I caught her pouring cranberry juice into her Crispix. So I said, "Virginia, you poured cranberry juice into your Crispix." And she looks down into the bowl and it registers that she poured cranberry juice into her Crispix. So she dumps the whole thing into the garbage disposal, goes to the dish drainer, gets a new bowl, and I'm standing there grinding coffee right—

ELLIOT: Right.

JEFF: And the thing is going, "Vrrr, Vrrr, Vrrr, Vrrr."

ELLIOT: You can't hear her.

JEFF: Yeah. No. I mean, no I can't hear her. But that's not the point. The point is that I was distracted.

ELLIOT: Right.

JEFF: Right. So, "Vrrrr, Vrrrr, Vrrrr." And I look over at Virginia.

ELLIOT: And she's eating out of the garbage disposal?

JEFF: No—she's. Elliot. Stop guessing. I'm going to tell you. You don't have to guess.

ELLIOT: I was just trying to reciprocate. To show I'm listening.

JEFF: O K, but you also derailed the entire story.

ELLIOT: I'm sorry, Jeff.

JEFF: Um. So… Wait. What was I saying?

ELLIOT: "Vrrrr, Vrrrr, Vrrrr."   JEFF: Right. Right. So I
                                     look back over at her.
                                     And she's doing it again.

ELLIOT: Cranberry juice?

JEFF: In her Crispix. So I said, "Virginia, what are you thinking about?" And do you know what she said?

(ELLIOT *starts to guess.*)

JEFF: *Don't* guess—I'm going to tell you.
"I keep seeing my Mom with another man. He's older.
And she's kissing his neck."

(CHARLOTTE *appears. She is college-aged and in
bellbottoms.*)

(*A* MAN *[LUCAS] stands behind her, his arms encircling
her. He kisses her neck.*)

JEFF: "And this man begins to run his hands over her
body."

(*The* MAN *does so.*)

JEFF: "And I've never seen my mother so happy."

(*Silence.* CHARLOTTE *and the* MAN *disappear.*)

(ELLIOT *picks up his seltzer and drinks. He returns the drink
to the table.*)

ELLIOT: Wow. It's weird how her Mom doesn't stop
with this guy if Virginia is standing there watching.

JEFF: No. It was a DREAM, man. But then, in the
morning, she said she saw it AGAIN. But this time, she
wasn't sleeping. It was, I dunno, like a… "vision" or
something.

ELLIOT: Vision?

JEFF: I dunno what you'd call it.

ELLIOT: That's messed up. That's like, um, Oedipus or
Freud or something.

JEFF: Thanks for your diagnosis, Elliot.

ELLIOT: Yeah.

(JEFF *takes a sip of his beer.*)

ELLIOT: Why are these chairs so low?

(JEFF *is looking at someone in the bar.*)

JEFF: Hey, you see her?

ELLIOT: Who? Her?

JEFF: Don't you dare point.

ELLIOT: I wasn't gonna point.

JEFF: You were gonna point.

ELLIOT: She's cute.
I like pigtails.

JEFF: She keeps looking over here.

ELLIOT: Do you know her?

JEFF: I don't think so.
How's Hannah?

ELLIOT: Good. Probably… She dumped me.

JEFF: What? When?

ELLIOT: Two nights ago. She told me she just wants
to be my "friend". I told her I already have "friends."
What I don't have is a *girl*friend. She said that she…
wanted to take some time off from dating. So she can
focus on her custom jewelry business.

JEFF: I'm sorry, man. How long did you see her?

ELLIOT: Five months.
Well… Like almost four months.
She also got mad when I tried to guess what she was
going to say next.

JEFF: I'm sorry, man.

ELLIOT: It's my lisp.

JEFF: It's not your lisp.

ELLIOT: It's my confidence.

JEFF: It might be your confidence.

(ELLIOT *smiles a little.*)

ELLIOT: Jeff, what's wrong with me? Would you please just tell me? I feel like, like I've heard whispering behind my back my whole life.

JEFF: No one's whispering—

ELLIOT: I really, like, I really wanted it to work. I'm blowing through years of my life that could be filled with happiness. Always thinking…O K…just get through it, Elliot; just get through it and eventually stuff will get better.
But it doesn't.
It's like I'm trying to get to this mythical strip of land somewhere in the future. And no matter how fast and how far I run, it keeps getting further away.

JEFF: Farther. Farther away.

ELLIOT: Further.

(JEFF *shakes his head "no".*)

(*Silence*)

JEFF: You'll meet someone. I bet your future wife is somewhere eating a sandwich right now.

ELLIOT: Or getting fucked by another guy.
I think you're only happy when I'm a mess.

(*Silence*)

JEFF: Why does that girl keep looking over here?
O K. You want to know?

ELLIOT: What?

JEFF: What's wrong with you. Do you actually want to know? You're depressed.

ELLIOT: So?

JEFF: So, it's depressing. Girls don't want to have to, like, jazz-i-fy your spirits every time they see you. Girls want to fall in love.

ELLIOT: I've got a lot to be depressed about. I don't have any money. I hate my job. I don't have a girlfriend. I don't have anything to look forward to. I was an *alcoholic*.

JEFF: You're not an alcoholic. You had *one* bad night in college and made an ass of yourself.

ELLIOT: But there's a *history* of substance abuse in my family. My *grandmother* was…extremely obese.

JEFF: Fine, man. Call yourself whatever you want, but don't offer it to girls *up* front. I've *heard you do it!* "Hey, you're cute. I'm Elliot. I'm a recovering alcoholic. You look smart. Can I buy you a beer and watch you drink it?"

ELLIOT: I don't say that.

JEFF: (*Like it's a grand secret of dating*) Don't have any expectations. Just talk to her. Don't show you're interested. Just talk to her. And then, while you're talking, she'll be thinking, "Wait. Why *isn't* this guy hitting on me? Am I not as attractive as I thought? Do I have like boogers hanging out of my nose? Does *he* think I'm not good enough for *him*?"

ELLIOT: She will?

JEFF: Absolutely.

ELLIOT: That's not how you got Virginia.

JEFF: Well with Virginia I *knew*.

ELLIOT: No man, *I* knew. She wore those green socks and I kept telling you about —

JEFF: Green socks?

ELLIOT: Yeah, but you —

JEFF: The point *is* with Virginia it was so easy. I just
asked her out and she said, "Sure".
And then marriage. Will you marry me? … "Sure".
With Virginia it's just…easy.
(Silence)
That girl is staring at you. Go introduce yourself.

ELLIOT: *(He's terribly nervous)* All right. I will.

JEFF: Good. But wipe the sweat off your upper lip.
Fix your hair.

ELLIOT: What's wrong with it?

JEFF: It just…I dunno. Just like, move it around.

ELLIOT: Like this?

JEFF: Yeah…I guess. And unbutton your shirt a button.
No, not from the bottom. The top button. Unbutton
that.

(ELLIOT does so.)

ELLIOT: Do I look ok?

JEFF: Yeah. You look good. And remember…she's
looking for someone too. You're not trying to trick her.
Elliot. You're a great guy.

ELLIOT: Can I hug you?

JEFF: …ehhhhh…fine.

(They hug. Over ELLIOT's shoulder, JEFF sees something.)

JEFF: Elliot!! Um…behind. Ah shit. Behind. Um. Behind
that girl I just saw Hannah.

ELLIOT: What?? She's here? I should go talk to her.
(He re-buttons his top button, frantically.)

JEFF: No, man. She's…

(ELLIOT *is craning his neck. He takes a step back,
heartbroken.*)

ELLIOT: Who's that guy? I've never seen that guy
before.
Who's that guy? And why is she making out with him?

JEFF: She looks...*drunk.*

ELLIOT: She never kissed me in public. Said P D A
made her want to vomit.

JEFF: Maybe she'll vomit in his mouth. Or his ear. Or
his...

(ELLIOT *and* JEFF *both tilt their heads simultaneously,
watching.*)

ELLIOT & JEFF: Whoa.

4

(CHARLOTTE *sits with* VIRGINIA's *street clothes and
cellphone. She holds up the orange sweatshirt.*)

CHARLOTTE: *(Calling off)* Is this the famous orange
sweatshirt that brought you and Jeff together?

VIRGINIA: *(Off)* Umm...yeah.

CHARLOTTE: It's all pilly.
What button do I press to get to the camera?

VIRGINIA: *(Off)* I don't know.

CHARLOTTE: I don't see why
they hide it... Is this the—
Oh! Which button, Ginny?
I want to get a shot of this   VIRGINIA: *(Off)* I don't
for your dad...   know.

Uh-oh, I think it's recording

video. Hello?

> This dress makes my
> arms look weird.

CHARLOTTE: *(Giving up on the camera phone)* You have great arms! Your arms are my arms.

VIRGINIA: *(Off)* Fine, but I have Dad's boobs.

CHARLOTTE: *(Laughing)* Oh honey, he's been jogging again. Be nice.

VIRGINIA: *(Off)* You be nice.

CHARLOTTE: Come out of there already—I wanna…

(VIRGINIA enters wearing a wedding dress.)

(She looks spectacular.)

(CHARLOTTE, for the first time, maybe ever, is speechless.)

CHARLOTTE: You look beautiful, Ginny.

VIRGINIA: *(Trying not to give her mother the satisfaction, but she smiles too.)* What else would a mother say?

CHARLOTTE: You look beautiful. She did a beautiful job. You wear it better than I ever did.

VIRGINIA: What is the point of this thing anyway? If *white* means it's a purity dress, then let me tell you, Mommy Dearest, the whole dress should be a tasteful *black*.

CHARLOTTE: And I am closing my ears…

VIRGINIA: What? You don't actually think that Jeff and I are still—

CHARLOTTE: Just…just don't speak that way in front of your father.

VIRGINIA: Well, tell Dad that when Jeff and I hold hands, he always wear rubber gloves.

CHARLOTTE: Annnnnnnnnd let's change the subject.

VIRGINIA: When did you lose your virginity?

(Silence)

CHARLOTTE: What?

VIRGINIA: Dad thinks you were a virgin when you guys got married.

CHARLOTTE: He. Um. He. Why do you…I don't want to—

VIRGINIA: It's obvious. And I've seen photos of him back then. He was a total nerd.

CHARLOTTE: No he wasn't. He was—

VIRGINIA: And you looked hot.

CHARLOTTE: *Looked?*

VIRGINIA: So were you?

CHARLOTTE: Turn.

VIRGINIA: You're not going to answer?
Mom?

CHARLOTTE: Have you thought about the shoes?

VIRGINIA: The shoes?

CHARLOTTE: Yes. I don't think we should keep the ones you have at home. If you buy something for your wedding because it's on sale, it doesn't bode well.

VIRGINIA: Did you have serious relationships before Dad?

CHARLOTTE: What?for the marriage.

VIRGINIA: Before Dad.

CHARLOTTE: I dated. Turn again. I want to get a shot from the side.

VIRGINIA: Did anyone break your heart?

CHARLOTTE: Has Jeff settled on a suit?

VIRGINIA: Why won't you answer me?

CHARLOTTE: Because I…don't want to.

VIRGINIA: Why? You don't want to? What kind of answer is that?

CHARLOTTE: It's my answer.

VIRGINIA: Which is not an answer. What's the big deal? My friends talk with their parents about these things.

CHARLOTTE: People do things different ways.

VIRGINIA: "People do things different ways"? What does that even mean?

CHARLOTTE: You just want to embarrass me.

VIRGINIA: I don't. I want to know you. I feel like I don't actually KNOW you.

CHARLOTTE: Glad to hear the last twenty-odd years had no affect on you—

VIRGINIA: I mean KNOW you.

CHARLOTTE: Change.

VIRGINIA: Why can't we just talk like two people?

CHARLOTTE: Because we're not BUDDIES, Virginia.

(Silence)

VIRGINIA: Well, how did you *know* that you wanted to marry Dad?

CHARLOTTE: He worked at the Julliard bookstore.

VIRGINIA: I know the fairy tale. I need to know if you ever had doubts.

CHARLOTTE: Everyone has doubts. It's totally normal, sweetheart. But Jeff is an incredible guy. He's handsome and he cares about you—

VIRGINIA: Are you telling me that you never loved anybody else?
You never had a specific person in mind that you wanted to marry instead of Dad?

(A man appears. It's 1970.)

MAN: (LUCAS) Charlotte. I usually hate movies, let alone one about a planet full of monkeys, but…that was fun. *Fun.* That's a word I don't say very often. *Fun.* Until I met you, I didn't think it was possible for things to get better.
(He exits.)

(Silence)

VIRGINIA: How do I know I'm not going to regret this?

CHARLOTTE: Take that off. You'll stain the armpits.

(VIRGINIA starts to undress.)

CHARLOTTE: Dad is bringing home Chinese. He wants me to find out what you two want.

VIRGINIA: What I want?
Doesn't matter.

CHARLOTTE: What does Jeff want?

VIRGINIA: What does Jeff want?
Hell if I know.
(She exits.)

(The lights fade.)

5

(Morning)

(CHRISTOPHER *and* JEFF *are jogging.*)

(CHRISTOPHER *and* JEFF *heavy breathing*)

CHRISTOPHER: It's good. Jeff. That you. That you
wanted to. Exercise.

JEFF: Yeah. Well.

CHRISTOPHER: Every. Morning. Three. Miles.

JEFF: You. Run. In the. Snow?

CHRISTOPHER: No.

(Jogging)

CHRISTOPHER: Important to. Stay in shape.
So Charlotte. Doesn't. Leave me.

(JEFF *laughs.*)

JEFF: Leaves. Starting to. Change.

CHRISTOPHER: I love the. Crunch!
Crunch! Crunch! Crunch!

(Jogging)

JEFF: Can we. Can we stop a minute?
(He stops jogging.)

(CHRISTOPHER *jogs back to* JEFF.)

CHRISTOPHER: Tired already? Man, I'm in great shape!

JEFF: Well…I'm not tired exactly.

(CHRISTOPHER *starts to stretch.*)

JEFF: I'm worried about Virginia.

CHRISTOPHER: She was always moody.

JEFF: No I know.

CHRISTOPHER: But she's worth it.

JEFF: No I know.
She's been calling all these retirement homes. Like every retirement home in the northeast.

CHRISTOPHER: I'm sure she wants to unload us.

JEFF: It's weird.
And she hasn't been. Um. She hasn't been sleeping well.

CHRISTOPHER: Charlotte didn't sleep a full month before the wedding. By the time we got to Dublin for the honeymoon, all she wanted to do was sleep. And by sleep, I actually mean sleep. And this is a girl who had never gone to bed with anybody... Too much information.
Suffice it to say it wasn't a real honeymoon until twenty minutes before we grabbed a cab to the airport.

JEFF: Virginia claims she's seeing these, like, visions.

CHRISTOPHER: Ah, "Like Visions". What's with your generation's ardent insistence on being imprecise?

JEFF: I said "she's been seeing visions".
(Silence)
Does she...is there a history of mental illness in your family?

CHRISTOPHER: O K, why don't we head back to the house now...

JEFF: Wait. I didn't mean for it to sound like that.

CHRISTOPHER: Virginia didn't really date any boys in high school.
(Silence)
Virginia was different from Luke. Her brother. Always. Luke was always wanting things. A magic kit. Bicycles. Rollerblades. Microscope. Computer. Another computer. Another computer. Another computer...

JEFF: Mister—

CHRISTOPHER: Virginia, well, you should have seen Charlotte and me in the toy store. Birthdays for Virginia were impossible. Christmas, forget about it. We'd just pick out things at random and give them to her. And she'd take them. And play them with them. Until we gave her something else.
The only thing she ever asked for was a camera.
I thought she liked capturing moments. Freezing time. Make things last. Make people see things in a new way.
I once asked her why she liked taking pictures.
You know what she said?
She liked the sound.
Of the shutter.

JEFF: I don't know what you're trying to say to me or—

CHRISTOPHER: Jeff. I've known Virginia much longer than you.
I've known her much, much longer than you. And I see both of you together staying at the house…

JEFF: What are you saying?

CHRISTOPHER: The girl is lost. She doesn't know what she wants.
(Silence)
When I met Charlotte I knew that she loved me.
You just know, Jeff. It's something you just know.
I don't doubt that you feel very strong things for her. I don't doubt it.
But the girl doesn't know what love is.
(Silence)

JEFF: With all due respect—

CHRISTOPHER: Oh I hoped no one would ever use that phrase on me—

JEFF: You're wrong.
Sir.

(A long pause)

CHRISTOPHER: How many times have you been in love?

JEFF: I don't know.

CHRISTOPHER: How many women have you told you loved them? Not including your mother. Or sister.

JEFF: I don't have a sister.

CHRISTOPHER: How many?

JEFF: I don't know.
(He thinks for a while.)
Five?
(No response)
O K. So. How about you?

CHRISTOPHER: One.
I'll see you back at the house.
(He jogs away.)

6

(At the gallery)

(ELLIOT looks at slides.)

(VIRGINIA stands, holding a cup of coffee.)

VIRGINIA: My Mom and Dad are like partners or, sort of, coworkers in life. But the person I keep seeing when I close my eyes is DIFFERENT. She's rebellious and fragile and…she wants things so deeply.
She's SURE of what she wants. She KNOWS it. And…
and I get there are no guarantees, but I wonder…I don't know. I think maybe I just need to relax.

ELLIOT: I think it's just the stress of the wedding.

VIRGINIA: I think I'm broken.

ELLIOT: You're not broken.

VIRGINIA: What are your parents like?

ELLIOT: My parents used to walk around the house naked. They'd make out at Thanksgiving dinner. It was awful. I'd have to say, "Dad, please let go of Mom and cut the turkey."

VIRGINIA: Have you ever been in love?

ELLIOT: I mean. Well.

VIRGINIA: Oh right. Hannah.

ELLIOT: Oh I didn't love her. Hannah. Ugh. Her name alone makes me want to kill myself. And if I did kill myself, Hannah'd probably tell people, "Oh, once a man fell in love with me so deeply that he killed himself over me." She'd probably use me as a pick-up line.

VIRGINIA: It's just…I saw myself in her wedding dress and…I guess it should have scared me to death, but it didn't. I kept trying to stop myself from smiling. I didn't want my Mom to see.

ELLIOT: Why?

VIRGINIA: …I don't know.
Do you hear that knocking?

(*A sudden light shift and loud knocking. A bespectacled man,* LUCAS, *sits on a piano bench in a practice room. reading a newspaper. He looks up at the knocking.*)

MAN: Come in.

(CHARLOTTE *enters. She's 20. She wears 70s bellbottoms and a knit top.*)

MAN: Charlotte.

VIRGINIA: No!

CHARLOTTE: I've come for my lesson.

MAN: *(Checks his watch)* You're forty minutes early.

CHARLOTTE: I need extra help. If that's O K. If you're busy...

ELLIOT: Virginia?

(The MAN considers. He shifts over on the bench. CHARLOTTE sits beside him.)

VIRGINIA's head bolts upright.

VIRGINIA: No!

ELLIOT: No...what? You don't like this one?

MAN: Where did we leave off?

CHARLOTTE: With the chorales...

MAN: Have you been practicing your fingering?
(He outstretches his arms—his fingers falling on invisible piano keys.)

MAN: 5, 2, 4, 5, 2, 4...

(We hear music.)

(CHARLOTTE places her fingers on the keys.)

CHARLOTTE & MAN: 5, 2, 4, 5, 2, 4

VIRGINIA & CHARLOTTE & MAN: 5, 2, 4, 5, 2, 4...

(CHARLOTTE leans her head on his shoulder.)

CHARLOTTE: Lucas.

VIRGINIA: Oh God. It's him.

CHARLOTTE: I think your shoulder is the best place in the Universe.

ELLIOT: Glove, please.

CHARLOTTE: Please play me something.

MAN: Charlotte…

ELLIOT: Virginia, can you hand me the glove?

CHARLOTTE: Play for me.

ELLIOT: Okay, I'll get it.

CHARLOTTE: You don't have a wife, Lucas. You don't have kids. There's no good reason why we can't be together.

(LUCAS *sighs and starts to play Bach's "Chromatic Fantasia and Fugue in D minor". From memory.*)

CHARLOTTE: I'm an adult.

LUCAS: If you're an adult, than that makes me two-thirds decomposed.
You know…that's what Bach is doing right now. Decomposing…

CHARLOTTE: I love you.

VIRGINIA: *(Urgently.)*Talk to me, Elliot!

ELLIOT: I was talking to you.

	CHARLOTTE: I'm in love with you.
VIRGINIA: Tell me the most interesting thing you know.	
	CHARLOTTE: Did you hear
Elliot!	what I said?
ELLIOT: I'm thinking!	
VIRGINIA: Just say anything!	
Talk!!	CHARLOTTE: Lucas?

ELLIOT: Beware the Jabberwock, my son. The

jaws that bite, the claws
that catch.

VIRGINIA: *(Yelling at*   ELLIOT: Beware the
CHARLOTTE.) You don't   Jubjub bird…
love him!

CHARLOTTE: Lucas?

LUCAS: I heard you.   ELLIOT: Virginia?

CHARLOTTE: I'll take Theory from someone else. You're
barely even my professor.
I can't sleep. I can't eat a thing. At least that'll please
my mother.

ELLIOT: Virginia?

CHARLOTTE: Can you hear   ELLIOT: Can you hear
me?   me?

ELLIOT: Tell me what you want. I'll do it.

LUCAS: I want you. Only you. For the first time in thirty
years I—

CHARLOTTE: And I want you.

VIRGINIA: This is—

ELLIOT: This is?

CHARLOTTE: This is perfect. How often in life does this
happen?

LUCAS: I'm an old man.

CHARLOTTE: You're not old.

LUCAS: I'm fifty-seven years old, Charlotte.

CHARLOTTE: And you fuck me like you're nineteen.

VIRGINIA: Lucas!

ELLIOT: What?

VIRGINIA: Elliot! Elliot! Elliot! Elliot!

ELLIOT: I have no idea what is happening right now!!

(LUCAS *pauses his playing a moment. Then resumes.*)

CHARLOTTE: I want to feel your legs against mine
again. I want to lie with my head on your chest, staring
across your bedroom at the spines of all your. I want
to feel your heart rise as you tell me about the first
performance of *The Rite of Spring*.

LUCAS: People hated it so much fist fights broke out.
Imagine that happening today. I turn on the radio and
I'd rather hear static. Where are our geniuses?

CHARLOTTE: You're the genius. To hear you play…

LUCAS: The distance between Good and Great is the
thickness of a razorblade. My *hand*.

CHARLOTTE: Put it in my mouth.

VIRGINIA: Talk!

ELLIOT: As Mayor of the Munchkin City. In the County
of the Land of Oz.

CHARLOTTE: I want to taste you.

(CHARLOTTE *puts her hand in* LUCAS's *lap.*)

VIRGINIA: Ohhhhh!

ELLIOT: We welcome you most regally. But we've got
to verify it legally.

LUCAS: You should hear yourself…

(LUCAS *puts* CHARLOTTE's *hand on her lap.*)

VIRGINIA: Ohhhhh!

ELLIOT: (*Overlapping*) To see if she is morally, ethically,
spiritually, physically…

VIRGINIA: Ohhhhh!

ELLIOT: Positively, absolutely…

CHARLOTTE: I will never love anyone else but you. I know it.

VIRGINIA: Ohhhhh!

ELLIOT: Undeniably and reliably—

(VIRGINIA *grabs* ELLIOT *and kisses him. The kiss is passionate and long. His arms are outstretched—he will not be an active participant. Slowly, though, he begins to give in. His arms start to encompass her. One on the back of her neck. And one on the back of her waist.*)

(LUCAS *slams the keys.*)

LUCAS: I'm fifty-seven years old!

CHARLOTTE: Lucas, I *love* you. I've never felt anything like this before.
I only thought I did.
You really do know it when you feel it.
And I feel it.
Don't you?
God. Why aren't you talking?
I know you do.
Lucas?
Lucas just say it!

(*Silence*)

LUCAS: I…I have…I forgot about a dental appointment that was… Took me weeks to get…

(*Silence*)

(*Then,* CHARLOTTE *stands up.*)

CHARLOTTE: You WANT to be unhappy. You are a miserable, HOPELESS person.
And you will never be able to forget me. Never. You will regret this day for the rest of your life, Lucas.
More, much more than the day you cut your finger.

So you won't be a concert pianist, but at least you can
still play.
What we have you will never be able to have again.
You hear me?! This will be the biggest regret of your
entire life—

LUCAS: I know it.
But...
This too shall pass.

(A moment of consideration)

CHARLOTTE: Aw go to hell.

(Door slams.)

(LUCAS takes off his glasses. He rubs his eyes.)

(Lights fade on LUCAS.)

(Slowly, VIRGINIA stops kissing ELLIOT. She backs away.)

(ELLIOT looks like he's been hit by a truck.)

ELLIOT: Virginia...

(VIRGINIA starts to pack her bag.)

ELLIOT: What are you doing?
Where are you going? It's only...it's only 11:30?
Why did you...why did you kiss me, Virginia?

(VIRGINIA puts on her coat.)

ELLIOT: I don't understand. I never understand.

(VIRGINIA heads for the door.)

ELLIOT: Wait!

(VIRGINIA turns.)

ELLIOT: I just wanted to tell you...
That I saw you first.
Ask him. I called you "Socks" because I once saw you
wear these bright green knee-high socks. I'd say, "I

saw Socks in the library." And "I saw Socks in Pizza
Palace. I think she was looking at me."
It's dumb…

(Silence)

VIRGINIA: I remember those socks.

ELLIOT: I saw you first. It's not like calling shotgun, I
know it doesn't work that way, but…
I think you're perfect, Virginia.
And every day it kills me because I know you just said
yes to Jeff because he asked.
And every day it kills me because I wish I'd had the
guts to.

(VIRGINIA exits.)

7

(In the Julliard Bookstore, hours after the previous scene.
CHRISTOPHER, *in 70s garb, alphabetizes L Ps.)*

(A light up on VIRGINIA. *In a daze, she watches…)*

CHRISTOPHER: *(Calling offstage to someone behind him*
in the storeroom) No, Karl, I think you're wrong there.
Girls like to feel empowered these days. They'll respect
you more if you let THEM pay for dinner. And the
movie. And the cab.
Someday. If I'm ever with a girl, I'm just gonna sit
back and let her express her feminism. It's gonna be
awesome.
Romance is dead. Politics is king—EQUALITY, Karl,
no—not even equality—lopsided anti-chauvinism
or—I don't know the exact term but women are
mentally *better* than *men.* It's science. It's in *Newsweek*
for heck's sake.

Science proves it and you and me, Karl, we get to
benefit up the wazoo because women'll pay for stuff.
Tides are turning, Karl. Soak it up. It's a new frontier
out there.

Karl?

Are you still here?

(CHARLOTTE *enters the store. She's wearing what she
wore in the previous scene. She looks upset, but is trying to
conceal it.*)

CHRISTOPHER: Charlotte.

CHARLOTTE: Hi, Christopher.

CHRISTOPHER: Are you O K?
So…what can I get you?
(*Looks at the L P in his hand.*)
Might you be shoppin' for some shoppin?

CHARLOTTE: Show-pan.

CHRISTOPHER: I know. I was trying to make you laugh.
Trying to make a Chopin joke.

CHARLOTTE: A bunch of the woodwinds are having a
party tonight and I wondered if you wanted to go.

CHRISTOPHER: With you?

CHARLOTTE: That's the idea.

CHRISTOPHER: Um. I'm supposed to have dinner
tonight with my Aunt in Ronkonkoma.

CHARLOTTE: O K, well, maybe another…

CHRISTOPHER: Wait. No. Yes. Of course. Idiot! Yes,
Charlotte. Yes. I'd love to go to dinner with you if the
offer still—

CHARLOTTE: It's not dinner, it's a party, but. Yeah. O K. Pick me up at nine. Lemme tell you where I live. My dorm is—

CHRISTOPHER: Nine at night?

CHARLOTTE: Actually. Instead of telling you where I live, let's just meet here at nine.
(Silence)
Can you give me some sort of verbal response?

CHRISTOPHER: Yes.

CHARLOTTE: I'll see you tonight.
(She starts to exit.)
Oh. And…see if you have any time to change.
(She exits.)

(CHRISTOPHER is dumbstruck.)

CHRISTOPHER: See you tonight.
KARL!

(Lights fade.)

8

(JEFF enters in a towel. A toothbrush sticks out of his mouth. He walks over to a table and picks up the remote. He turns on the television. It's the Weather Channel.)

(VIRGINIA is sitting on the bed, unbeknownst to JEFF.)

(JEFF turns and sees VIRGINIA.)

JEFF: Jesus Christ!!

VIRGINIA: Hi, Jeff.

JEFF: …Hi.
(Silence)
How…was work?

VIRGINIA: I came home early.

JEFF: Yeah.

VIRGINIA: Are you watching the Weather Channel?

JEFF: Huh?

(VIRGINIA *gestures to the television.*)

JEFF: Oh. Yeah. I guess so.

VIRGINIA: I've seen this one. The ending is really predictable.

JEFF: Is this the one where Day becomes Night?

VIRGINIA: Yeah. The sun is, apparently, going to set…

(JEFF *walks over to* VIRGINIA *and starts to kiss her. She kisses him back. After a few kisses, he stops.*)

JEFF: You're not stopping.

VIRGINIA: No, you are.

JEFF: Yeah, that's because I'm a fucking moron.

(JEFF *and* VIRGINIA *kiss again.*)

JEFF: You've not let me touch you for like a month.

VIRGINIA: Touch me.

(JEFF *puts his hand on* VIRGINIA*'s breast.*)

VIRGINIA: That's my boob.

JEFF: I know.

VIRGINIA: You need to cut your nails.

JEFF: Huh? Oh yeah. I…I will.

(*Silence, except for The Weather Channel.*)

VIRGINIA: So…are we going to have sex or not?

JEFF: You came home from work to have sex with me?

VIRGINIA: Just kiss me.

(JEFF *kisses* VIRGINIA. *They move toward the bed. He kneels on it. They are still making out.*)

JEFF: *(Through kisses)* Virginia?

VIRGINIA: Mmmm.

JEFF: Virginia, I feel like you're not totally here.

VIRGINIA: Don't be a girl.

JEFF: Excuse me?

(VIRGINIA *pushes* JEFF *down on the bed.*)

VIRGINIA: Take your boxers off.

(JEFF *and* VIRGINIA *under the covers. He pulls off his boxers. She kisses him hard.*)

JEFF: Ow! Virginia. Slow down.
Please. Just. Haha. Just hold on there bucco.

VIRGINIA: *(Annoyed)* What?!

JEFF: What's happening right now?

VIRGINIA: If you need me to explain this to you—

JEFF: Look, this is fun. But…it's also weird. And sometimes weird can be fun. But right now, weird is just weird.

VIRGINIA: Just lean back and shut up.
(She goes under the covers.)

JEFF: Um. So…oh. Ohhhhh wow. So…I think we need to. Oh. O K. Talk.
In a. In a minute. Or.
I thought you hated doing this.

(Silence, except for the television.)

JEFF: Did you know it's gonna rain tomorrow?

(VIRGINIA'*s head comes back out.*)

VIRGINIA: Tell me you love me.

JEFF: I love you.

VIRGINIA: Tell me again.

JEFF: I love you.

VIRGINIA: Again.

JEFF: I LOVE you.

VIRGINIA: But how do you know?

JEFF: Because I know.
I love you.
(Something occurs to him.)
Virginia.
Tell me you love me.

(Silence)

VIRGINIA: *(While still straddling him)*
I need to tell you something.
I…
You know when the thermometer says you have a
fever but the room feels freezing even though it might
be, like, eighty degrees? So you put on every T-Shirt
you have. And then every sweater. And then every
coat. Till you're just lying on your bed, a big pile of
everything you own.

JEFF: O K.

VIRGINIA: And even though it's eighty degrees, it
doesn't change the fact that you still feel like it's ten
below.

JEFF: Are you cold?

VIRGINIA: I kissed Elliot.

JEFF: You—

VIRGINIA: I kissed Elliot.

(JEFF *pushes* VIRGINIA *off him. He pulls on his boxers and gets out of bed.*)

JEFF: Why'd you kiss him?

VIRGINIA: I don't know.

JEFF: Yes you do.

VIRGINIA: No I really don't.

JEFF: Did he kiss you back?

VIRGINIA: Not really.

JEFF: Did you have sex with him?

VIRGINIA: No.

JEFF: Did he like kissing you?

VIRGINIA: He—

JEFF: Did you like it?

VIRGINIA: Yes.

This stops JEFF.

JEFF: You know what. This is where you're supposed to lie.

VIRGINIA: I'm telling you the truth. Isn't that what's important?

JEFF: What's important...what's... This is fucking *bullshit!!*
(*He kicks the bed.*)
OW!!

VIRGINIA: Oh, you kicked the metal.

JEFF: I KNOW I KICKED THE METAL!

VIRGINIA: Please let's talk about this. I want to talk about this.
(*Pulls on the orange sweatshirt, but has trouble finding the head-hole.*)

JEFF: Yes, by all means, let's talk about this...maybe make some chamomile tea, have a good cry and...a good, nice long cry and...*where is the opening!!!*

VIRGINIA: My mother made the wrong choices. I can SEE it now. It's so obvious and...and I need to know what we are doing, what we'll HAVE is not what she has and—

JEFF: *(Gesturing to them, then to the parents room down the hall) This* has nothing to do with *that.*

VIRGINIA: Yes it does.

JEFF: You think I haven't noticed?

VIRGINIA: What?

JEFF: That you don't care about ANYTHING?

VIRGINIA: That's not true!

JEFF: Virginia, you haven't taken a photo of me in a year.

VIRGINIA: What?

JEFF: You used to take photos of me all the time. Of me sleeping. Of me eating. Of me walking around and doing dumb shit.
Something changed.

(A cell phone rings. JEFF and VIRGINIA ignore it.)

(VIRGINIA's eyes look over to the phone.)

JEFF: I don't know why. But I know WHEN.
It's when the photos stopped.
I guess...I guess I just thought you were going to start again.

(VIRGINIA walks over to the phone.)

JEFF: You're seriously gonna answer your phone now?

(VIRGINIA looks at the screen.)

VIRGINIA: Oh, Jesus, Jeff, hold on.

(JEFF *starts to protest as* VIRGINIA *answers.*)

VIRGINIA: "Hello?"
"This is she."
"Oh God."
"Are you sure?"
"No, no relation."
"How old is he?"
"O K. O K, thank you."
(*She hangs up. She is in a stunned silence.*)

JEFF: Who the hell was that?

VIRGINIA: Good Shepherd Retirement Home. Lucas
Schroeder is a real person.
My Mom married my Dad…out of…*spite.*

JEFF: Who the fuck cares if Lucas Schroeder is a real
person? This is about you and me.

VIRGINIA: *You* forced me into this. *You put all this…this
pressure* on me and…

JEFF: Holy shit—is this really your best argument?

VIRGINIA: How can you just know you love me?

(*Silence*)

JEFF: How can you just change your mind?

VIRGINIA: To change my mind meant I even felt
something in the first place.

(JEFF *exits.*)

9

(*Back in 1971*)

(CHARLOTTE *leans against a wall.* CHRISTOPHER *stands opposite her, his hand supporting him, beside her head. She smokes a joint.*)

(VIRGINIA, *from afar and in dim light, observes.*)

(*We hear George Harrison's* All Things Must Pass. *Loud*)

CHARLOTTE: Do you like reefer?

CHRISTOPHER: Reefers? I love them.

CHARLOTTE: What?

CHRISTOPHER: I love them!

CHARLOTTE: Do you want a hit?

CHRISTOPHER: Oh. Um. In a little. I had. I had a whole bunch of reefers before the party.

(CHARLOTTE *and* CHRISTOPHER *listen to the music.*)

CHARLOTTE: I love this song.

CHRISTOPHER: Me too.

CHARLOTTE: Who's your favorite Beatle?

CHRISTOPHER: John Lennon.

CHARLOTTE: Really?

CHRISTOPHER: I know! How original. That's like saying my favorite condiment is ketchup, huh?

CHARLOTTE: Did you just say condom mint?

CHRISTOPHER: Condom what? I said, "Condi*ment*."

CHARLOTTE: Condom mint? Like a mint condom?

CHRISTOPHER: Yes, I said Condom Mint. Because that makes a ton of sense.

CHARLOTTE: Condom mint? Why'd you say that?

CHRISTOPHER: I didn't…
(*He's frustrated.*)

CHARLOTTE: You're gonna get a wrinkle across your head.

Here.

(*She traces a finger across his forehead.*)

You know...you're actually sort of cute.

CHRISTOPHER: I think you're the most beautiful girl I've ever seen in my entire life.

CHARLOTTE: I've heard that one before.

CHRISTOPHER: I don't doubt it.

I can't believe I'm with you.

You are so, so beautiful.

Do you know the only thing that gets me out of bed is the hope I'll see you?

I can't believe I'm here with– Wow. I probably should stop talking.

I understand if you want to go home or—

(LUCAS *enters, looking frantic.* CHARLOTTE *makes eye contact with him. They stare for a moment.* CHARLOTTE *kisses* CHRISTOPHER. CHRISTOPHER *turns and looks at* LUCAS. *Then, he turns back to* CHARLOTTE.)

CHRISTOPHER: Do you know him?

(CHARLOTTE *shakes her head and kisses* CHRISTOPHER *again.* LUCAS *exits. When* CHARLOTTE *stops the kiss, she sees that* LUCAS *has left.*)

CHRISTOPHER: I can't believe...I've wanted that to happen for so long.

CHARLOTTE: (*Leaden*) Me too.

CHRISTOPHER: Hey. Um. Do you want to...do you want to...to go listen to records at my apartment?

CHARLOTTE: Yes.

CHRISTOPHER: I have an air popper and we can make—

CHARLOTTE: *(Almost angrily)* I already said, "Yes".

CHRISTOPHER: Oh… Wow. Don't go anywhere. I just
need to. Stay right there.
(He smiles.)
I'll just grab your coat.
(He runs off.)

10

(The gallery. ELLIOT *paces, he's on the phone. He takes
swigs from a pint of whiskey.)*

ELLIOT: *(Quickly)* And when I saw you, with…with
your arms around that…guy, I wanted to kill myself.
God, Hannah, I mean, he wasn't even that attractive. I
could only see the back of his head, but I've seen better
backs of heads. Still, guess what, Hannah? Guess what?
You make this really annoying noise when you lick
yogurt off a spoon.
(He imitates the sound four or five times.)

*(*JEFF *enters, unseen by* ELLIOT.*)*

ELLIOT: You broke my heart….Hey ya know what,
HANNAH…I hate that dumb tattoo you got on your
right shoulder. "A for Anarchy". I know I told you it
was cool, but it's actually really friggin stupid. What
kind of anarchist makes custom jewelry? You went
to Mount Holyoke for Christ's sake. Your Dad pays
your *VISA*. But what I'm calling to say is…*Hannah*…
someone can *like* me. Someone can find me *attractive*.
Someone can actually want to be with me. It doesn't
always have to be the other way around.
So…in conclusion, bend over, fuck yourself in the dick
and I wish you my best.

My number's the same if you want to call me back.
(*He ends the call and smiles.*)

(JEFF *applauds.* ELLIOT *turns, surprised.*)

ELLIOT: Oh hey um hey Jeff.

JEFF: Elliot! You stood up for yourself.

ELLIOT: Yeah, I guess I did.

JEFF: How great. My, my what a journey you've had.
When I first met you, you just sat in our dormroom on
Friday nights and played computer games, jerking off
to Japanese cartoons. But now...

ELLIOT: Have you...have you seen Virginia?

JEFF: Virginia? Vir-gin-ia? Mmmm...doesn't ring a bell
but now, Elliot. Elliot!! Look at you, my little, little
dove. You're telling off Hannah. You've conquered
your alcoholism. You're having sex with an engaged
woman...

ELLIOT: Virginia?

JEFF: Elliot, exactly how many engaged women are you
fucking?

ELLIOT: We didn't...*do it*. She just kissed me. Once.

JEFF: That's not what she told me.

ELLIOT: No?

JEFF: She said that you raped her.	ELLIOT: It was only one kiss and it— Wait—what??!!
Why did you rape my fiancé, Elliot?	Oh my God, Jeff, I didn't.

ELLIOT: I didn't.

JEFF: But she says you did.

ELLIOT: I didn't, we just kissed.

JEFF: She says you took advantage of her. Held her down on the light box.

ELLIOT: She's lying to you! The light table can't even support the bodyweight of a single person, let alone— look. It's not broken! This is proof!

JEFF: She's dead, Elliot.
(*Silence*)
Say something!!!

ELLIOT: Who's dead?

JEFF: Virginia is dead.
She called me, told me you raped her, and then she went home and dumped an entire bottle of Ambien down her throat.
By the time I got home...

(ELLIOT *sits down on the ground with his head in his hands.*)

ELLIOT: I didn't...Jeff. You have to understand...I was just looking at slides and then she grabbed me and kissed me. That was it. That was it. She just grabbed me and...she kissed me. I didn't touch her. I don't know why she told you that I...that I

JEFF: Raped. That you *raped* her.

ELLIOT: I didn't!! Stop saying that I did when I didn't!

JEFF: You did! Admit it! You had sex with her!

ELLIOT: I...I touched her back a little when we kissed.

JEFF: Yes. Yes! See! And then what did you do!?

(CHRISTOPHER *enters.*)

ELLIOT: That's it. I swear!
Oh my God. Mister. I am.

CHRISTOPHER: Elliot, right?

ELLIOT: Yes—sir. I am—I am so, so sorry.

JEFF: *(To* CHRISTOPHER*)* What do you want?

CHRISTOPHER: You ran out on Virginia.

ELLIOT: *(Runs over to* CHRISTOPHER.*)* Please forgive me!

CHRISTOPHER: What? What is he talking about?

ELLIOT: I had...I didn't do anything!

*(*JEFF *walks away from* CHRISTOPHER *and* ELLIOT.*)*

CHRISTOPHER: Jeff, what is he talking about?

*(*JEFF *motions to* ELLIOT, *"Tell him".)*

ELLIOT: She's...*dead.*

CHRISTOPHER: Who's dead?

ELLIOT: Virginia.

CHRISTOPHER: No she's not.

JEFF: I told him Virginia killed herself.

CHRISTOPHER: *(Turning to* JEFF*)* What did he do?

ELLIOT: What!?!? Why would you do that to me!?!?

JEFF: *(To* CHRISTOPHER*)* Virginia didn't tell you?

CHRISTOPHER: Virginia told me you two got in some
fight, you ran off, and that we should split up find you.
She and Charlotte are checking the train station. They
told me to come check here.
Well. I guess you're found.

ELLIOT: Virginia is... Alive?

ELLIOT: *(To* JEFF*)* I could hit you!

JEFF: No you couldn't. Give me this!

ELLIOT: No—

JEFF: I don't want you to actually hurt yourself…
Jesus…
(He takes the bottle from ELLIOT. *He takes a large swig.)*

CHRISTOPHER: *(To* JEFF*)* Look… You're obviously pretty
mixed up right now, but Virginia is really worried
about you. I don't blame her. This is not how an adult
behaves, Jeff. Why don't you get in the car, we'll go
home, I'll put on a pot of coffee and you and Virginia
can talk through whatever problems —

JEFF: She told me she didn't love me.

ELLIOT: What?

JEFF: She told me she never did.
But she wasn't saying it to hurt me.
She was just telling the truth.

CHRISTOPHER: Jeff—when I first met Charlotte, it was
love at first sight, but it doesn't work that way for
everyone.

JEFF: Oh stop with that bullshit.
Do you want to know something about your wife?
You're living in a dreamland— You wanna know who
called today?

ELLIOT: What are you talking —

CHRISTOPHER: Get in the car.

JEFF: Guess who the fuck *called* today!!!

(A moment)

CHRISTOPHER: Who??
Who?
(Silence)
Will you get in the damn car with me, Jeff?
Everything will be fine.

JEFF: How can you know that?
How can you know that everything will be *fine?*

(A long silence)

CHRISTOPHER: Because people like us need it to be.
(He exits.)

(A moment)

(Then, JEFF *follows.)*

11

*(*CHARLOTTE *and* VIRGINIA *walk down a short hallway of a retirement home.* VIRGINIA *is preoccupied with the sheet of paper, glancing at doors. This should mirror the first moment of the play, when* VIRGINIA *was looking for the right book.)*

CHARLOTTE: He wouldn't swipe the card. I don't think the man even spoke English. He just pointed at the sign—ten dollar minimum. And I explained, "Sir, credit card minimums are *illegal.* You have to run my card. It's in the contract you signed when you got the credit card machine in the first place. If you don't want Mastercard taking a cut, then make your store cash only—not my problem. And a ten-dollar minimum? That's a little absurd, no? After all, I just wanted an apple juice.
So…is he here?
I didn't know Jeff volunteered at a retirement home.

VIRGINIA: He doesn't.

CHARLOTTE: What? What do you mean he doesn't?

VIRGINIA: We're not here for Jeff. We're here for you.

CHARLOTTE: *Ginny.* I may be old but I'm not *that* old.

(A beep. CHARLOTTE *pulls out her cell phone and opens it.)*

CHARLOTTE: Ah! Your father has sent me a textmail. Hooray! He found Jeff at the gallery. They're on their way home.
How neat. My first textmail.

VIRGINIA: They're just called "texts," Mom.

CHARLOTTE: Fine, fine. You are so savvy, Ginny. Don't give me a hard time.

VIRGINIA: I know that you only asked Daddy out because you wanted to hurt Lucas Schroeder.

CHARLOTTE: Lucas—

VIRGINIA: He's real. He's a real person.

CHARLOTTE: We're leaving. You are being *insufferable!* Honestly, Ginny. This is not like you.

VIRGINIA: Why is that a problem? Why can't I say what I actually THINK? What you actually think? What's gonna happen?

CHARLOTTE: Give me the keys.

VIRGINIA: You told Daddy you were a virgin when you married him but I bet you slept with at least—

CHARLOTTE: Give me the keys.

VIRGINIA: No.

CHARLOTTE: Give me the keys—I'm not discussing these subjects with my daughter.

VIRGINIA: Why? Are you afraid we'll have a real conversation?
You give me money. You make sure I get my flu shot. But you never wanted me to actually know you.
I don't want what you and Dad have. I want something

real.

I want to *know* that what I *have* is *real* love.

CHARLOTTE: Our marriage is *real*, Virginia. This is what
a long marriage *looks like*. This is what real, lasting love
looks like. You only notice the bad things. You *want* to
be angry.

VIRGINIA: But I have seen the truth, Mom. I know
things you never told me. I saw that everything
between you and Dad was based on a lie.
Admit it!
Why won't you admit it!!
(Silence)
Lucas Schroeder.

(Silence)

CHARLOTTE: What about him?

VIRGINIA: He's real.

CHARLOTTE: I know that.

(Silence)

VIRGINIA: So you admit —

CHARLOTTE: I said, "What about him?"

VIRGINIA: Do you still think about him?

CHARLOTTE: Hardly ever.
Hardly ever.
(A moment)
Sometimes I wonder.

VIRGINIA: You think about him every day.

CHARLOTTE: *(For the first time, really losing it)* You *don't*
know what I think!

VIRGINIA: You wish you married him.

CHARLOTTE: No I certainly don't.

VIRGINIA: You gave up music to put Dad through school—

CHARLOTTE: I didn't even *like* the French horn, sweetie. I didn't even like it. It was just something I did.

VIRGINIA: But you didn't *love* Dad.

CHARLOTTE: I grew to love him.

VIRGINIA: Grew to?

CHARLOTTE: Yes, grew to.

VIRGINIA: So you call that a life?

CHARLOTTE: You're damn right I do and you are not entitled to my *past*. It's mine. And it's passed.
Virginia—I am *not* like your friends' parents. You want me to hug you and promise that I can see something you can't?
I can't.
You want me to tell you that I KNOW every decision you make is right because I'm your Mom?
I won't.
I thought I raised you better than this.
You go around crying about wanting to fall in love?
Fall in it! Like it's some…*puddle*.
You've got a nice boy who wants to go through "what I call a life" with you. With *you*.
So for God's sake make a choice, be stronger, I love you so much Virginia, but please dear, really, *grow up*.
Now *give me the keys*.

(A door opens. LUCAS, a wilted, elderly man, stands before them.)

LUCAS: Yes, hello? Are you singers?
(Silence)
Were you singing?

CHARLOTTE: Lucas.
Lucas.

(CHARLOTTE *hugs* LUCAS.)

LUCAS: Are you here to sing?

CHARLOTTE: No...Lucas. Do you know who I am?

LUCAS: No.

CHARLOTTE: Charlotte. It's me, Charlotte!
I played the French horn.
You taught me at Juilliard.

LUCAS: (*An easy happiness—like finding a dollar bill*) I taught at Juilliard? Well isn't that something.

CHARLOTTE: You...you are a pianist.

LUCAS: Well isn't that something.
(*He smiles broadly.*)

(*Silence*)

CHARLOTTE: This...is Virginia. This is my daughter.

LUCAS: Hello, Virginia. You are a pretty girl. I...I...

CHARLOTTE: It's O K, Lucas.

LUCAS: (*Turning to* VIRGINIA, *confiding*) She thinks my name is *Lucas!*

(*A male* NURSE *walks through.* CHARLOTTE *stops him.*)

CHARLOTTE: Excuse me.
Does. Um. This is Lucas Schroeder, isn't it?

NURSE: This is Mister Schroeder.
Mister Schroeder, don't bother them!
He does this a lot...

CHARLOTTE: He's not bothering us...
How...how long has he been here?

NURSE: At least since I started working here, and that was four years ago. Do you know him?

CHARLOTTE: I was one of his students.

NURSE: He was a teacher? You were a teacher, Mister Schroeder! How about that!

LUCAS: Isn't that something!

CHARLOTTE: Does he still play the piano?

NURSE: The piano! Oh hell no. I didn't even know he was a teacher.

CHARLOTTE: He has no family?

NURSE: None that I know about. And he certainly doesn't know any.
Hey—Mister Schroeder—you got any family??

(LUCAS smiles and shrugs, sort of laughing.)

NURSE: A nice guy, though. One of the easier ones.

CHARLOTTE: Do you have a piano here?

NURSE: We got one in the chapel.

CHARLOTTE: Can we…

NURSE: Be my guest.
Field trip, Mister Schroeder!

LUCAS: Terrific!

(Django Reinhardt's 1938 recording of If I Had You *softly plays.)*

(JEFF enters and hesitantly approaches VIRGINIA. He pulls the orange sweatshirt off, placing it down.)

VIRGINIA: What are you doing here?
You stealin' my stuff?

JEFF: I was. Giving it back.

(*The lights fade up on* CHARLOTTE *and* LUCAS. *They sit, side-by-side, on a piano bench.*)

LUCAS: Are you going to play a song?

CHARLOTTE: I was hoping you would.

(LUCAS *laughs.*)

CHARLOTTE: You don't play the piano anymore?

LUCAS: You are…a *beautiful* woman.

(CHARLOTTE *laughs.*)

JEFF: So, Lucas Schroeder is down the hall with your Mom?

(VIRGINIA *nods.*)

JEFF: Maybe I'll move in here too. I'd have a cook, laundry, maid services. Lots of…newly eligible women.

(VIRGINIA *smiles.*)

(JEFF *sits down.*)

CHARLOTTE: I missed you.

LUCAS: That's nice.

CHARLOTTE: Will you put your fingers on the keys?

(LUCAS *puts one finger on the piano.*)

JEFF: Why did you want to get married to me?

VIRGINIA: Because you were cute. And you were nice to me. You made me laugh. And when you went away, I missed you.

JEFF: And that's not love?

(VIRGINIA *stares at* JEFF.)

JEFF: That's how I felt too.

VIRGINIA: Yeah?

JEFF: Yeah.

LUCAS: *(To* CHARLOTTE*)* Not much of a song, is it?

CHARLOTTE: Nothing? You don't remember how to play anything?

LUCAS: This too shall pass.

(A flicker of remembrance)

*(*CHARLOTTE *smiles.)*

JEFF: Do you...do you remember how we met?

VIRGINIA: You stole that out of my bag.

JEFF: Wait. You *knew* I did that?

*(*JEFF *and* VIRGINIA *laugh.)*

JEFF: Why'd you never tell me?

VIRGINIA: I dunno. It was a better story.

(Both sit on the bench. JEFF *stares out, wondering if* VIRGINIA *will say something next.* VIRGINIA *looks into her palm, wondering if* JEFF *will say something next.* JEFF *smiles.* VIRGINIA *smiles, looking away.)*

*(*CHARLOTTE *leans her head on* LUCAS*'s shoulder.)*

CHARLOTTE: Do you mind?

LUCAS: No, I don't mind.

CHARLOTTE: I just want to sit here a minute with you.

LUCAS: We can even sit for two minutes.

(The scene holds.)

(The scene fades.)

END OF PLAY

www.ingramcontent.com/pod-product-compliance
Lightning Source LLC
Chambersburg PA
CBHW052221090426
42741CB00010B/2630